BIRDS OF ANTARCTICA

ANTARCTICA

Lynn M. Stone

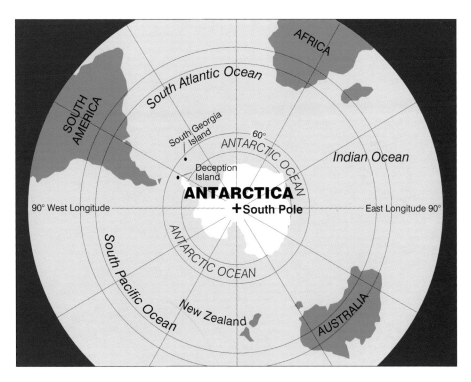

The Rourke Book Co., Inc.
Vero Beach, Florida 32964

PHOTO CREDITS
All photos © Lynn M. Stone except page 18 courtesy of U.S.
Geological Survey (W.B. Hamilton) and page 15 © Doug
Cheeseman

Library of Congress Cataloging-in-Publication Data

Stone, Lynn M.
    Birds of Antarctica / by Lynn M. Stone.
        p. cm. — (Antarctica)
    Includes index.
    ISBN 1-55916-141-8
    1. Sea birds—Antarctica—Juvenile literature.
2. Penguins—Antarctica—Juvenile literature.   [1. Sea birds
2. Penguins   3. Birds—Antarctica.]
I. Title II. Series: Stone, Lynn M.   Antarctica.
QL695.2.S88 1995
598.2998' 9—dc20   95–5985
                                                                      CIP
                                                                      AC

Printed in the USA

TABLE OF CONTENTS

BIRDS OF ANTARCTICA

Only 43 **species** (SPEE sheez), or kinds, of birds nest in the icy Antarctic region. Most of these species, though, exist in huge numbers! Perhaps 350 million birds live around Antarctica, and about half may be penguins.

Nearly all Antarctic birds are birds of the sea. Each spring and summer, though, they gather on the cold, rocky shores of Antarctica and its islands. The birds court each other, build nests, lay eggs and raise their chicks.

Nearly half of the millions of seabirds in the Antarctic region are penguins

WHERE THEY LIVE

Most of the Antarctic continent and its islands are covered by ice. No trees grow in the Antarctic area, and there is little ground free of ice and snow. Seabirds crowd together to nest on high beaches, cliffs and hillsides near the sea.

On islands some distance from Antarctica itself, birds nest among clumps of tussock grass.

Nearly all Antarctic birds spend much of their lives at sea.

Most Antarctic birds, such as these macaroni penguins, nest on cliffs or bare, rocky ground near the sea

WHAT THEY EAT

Seabirds eat seafood. Albatrosses, for example, catch fish, squid, and some of the tiny creatures that make up the ocean's **plankton** (PLANK ton).

The seven species of Antarctic penguins feed largely on plankton. Their most important plankton food is **krill** (KRILL).

The sheathbill, giant petrel and skua are **scavengers** (SKA ven jers). They eat dead animals and other leftovers. Skuas and giant petrels sometimes kill chicks, too.

Antarctica's blue-eyed shags dive for fish, which they grip with hooked bills

MAKING NESTS

In an icy, treeless land, Antarctic birds have to build simple nests on ground or rock. Nesting material is scarce. Some penguins solve that problem by making nests of pebbles!

Other birds use feathers, mud, moss and seaweed in their nests.

Emperor and king penguins don't build nests at all. Each father holds an egg on its feet. The dad can walk around while keeping the egg warm under a flap of loose belly skin.

Mother and father king penguins take turns keeping their one egg toasty on their feet.

A gentoo penguin carries a pebble stolen from another penguin's nest to its own

Master of flight, the black-browed albatross soars with ease over Antarctic seas

Not a beauty yet, a young wandering albatross grows up on South Georgia Island

RAISING YOUNG

Antarctic seabirds, like seabirds in other places, nest together in great flocks. These "villages" of nesting birds are **colonies** (KAH luh nees).

Most colonies have just one species of bird. Nearby, however, may be a colony of another species.

The chicks are raised within the colony. Parents feed their youngsters by coughing up part of the seafood in their stomachs.

By April or May the chicks of most species have grown up.

Young gentoo penguin begs food from a parent

HOW THEY LIVE

Nearly all Antarctic birds are designed for life at sea. Webbed feet are a must for swimming. Dense feathers are a must for protection from cold air and water. Penguins wear a layer of **blubber** (BLUH ber) for more warmth.

Each species has its own place in the Antarctic neighborhood. Different kinds of penguins, for example, hunt in different depths of seawater. In that way, one species does not crowd out another or take too much food from one place.

King penguins and other seabirds have waterproof raincoats of dense feathers

PENGUINS

Only seven of the world's eighteen species of penguins live in the Antarctic. Still, penguins are the best known Antarctic birds.

Penguins are seabirds that cannot fly. Their wings have no flight feathers.

Penguins use their wings like water paddles. They propel the penguins up to 15 miles per hour in the ocean!

Penguins stand up and walk like little people because their legs are set well to the rear of their bodies.

Antarctica's remarkable, deep-diving emperor penguins nest during the frigid Antarctic winter

TUBE-NOSED BIRDS

"Tube Nose" (TOOB NOZE) is the strange name that fits a whole group of Antarctica's birds. These birds have a hard, tubelike nostril on top of their upper bill.

Twenty-four kinds of tube noses, many of them called petrels, live in the Antarctic.

Petrels have long, narrow wings for their body size. They are excellent fliers. In flight they can pluck food from the ocean surface.

The "tube nose" of this nesting giant petrel may help the bird rid itself of extra salt

ALBATROSSES

The largest of the petrels are called albatrosses. They dip and turn gracefully in flight while rarely flapping their long wings.

Four species of albatrosses nest on islands in the Antarctic Ocean. The largest of them, the wandering albatross, is the world's largest seabird. The wanderer's wings stretch about 10 feet from tip to tip.

Courting albatrosses groom each other, coo, "dance," and clack their bills. That behavior earned them the nickname "gooney bird."

Glossary

blubber (BLUH ber) — a layer of fat which helps keep animals warm in cold climates

colony (KAH luh nee) — a group of animals of the same kind living together, especially to nest or raise young

krill (KRILL) — various shrimplike animals of cold seas

plankton (PLANK ton) — tiny, floating plants and animals of the seas and other bodies of water

scavenger (SKA ven jer) — an animal that feeds on dead animals and leftovers

species (SPEE sheez) — a certain kind of animal within a closely related group; for example, a *gentoo* penguin

tube nose (TOOB NOZE) — a group of seabirds with a hard, tubelike nostril on their upper bills; petrels, albatrosses and their relatives

INDEX